Life and Lemons

Life
and
Lemons

PRAGYA SINGH

To my heavenly mother, though you're not here,
your dreams live on in me.
You taught me to chase the light, to move with purpose,
and in every word I write, your courage speaks.
This is for you, and the fire you left in my soul.
Kumud Singh (25/06/1973-10/12/2020)
- P.S.

To those who have held my words close, who have seen
themselves in these lines, and who have reminded me
that poetry is never truly solitary, thank you. May you
find comfort, strength, and a piece of yourself within
these pages.

Table of Contents

SECTION I

Of Wounds and Shadows

There is a darkness that teaches.
A bruise that becomes a blueprint.

Here lie the poems born from ache,
of things left unsaid,
of lessons learned the hard way,
of wounds that whisper truths beneath their sting.

This is where the lemons first fell,
unripe and unforgiving.

To hush my wounds, to stand so tall.

The Weight of Their Wounds

I came with silence, a heart undone,
splintered by words like shards of sun.
The weight of their voice, sharp and cold,
pressed on my ribs, made sorrow bold.

Yet when I turned to let them see,
the ruin they carved so carelessly,
their lips trembled, their hands shook,
and suddenly, my pain was mistook.
Their sorrow poured like autumn rain,
as if their wounds eclipsed my pain.

And in their breaking, I was bound,
my grief dismissed, my arms around.
How cruel, this fate, to fold my ache,
to cradle ghosts my soul can't shake.
To hush my wounds, to stand so tall,
when all I wanted was to fall.

So here I sit, a quiet pyre,
burning alone, dousing their fire.
A ghost of sorrow, soft and mild,
once the hurt, now the child.

Pragya Singh

Let love shine through.

Aching Heart

My aching heart makes me write,
spilling sorrow into the night.
Everywhere is home, it's true,
just turn off the lights, let love shine through.

I promise you, come joy or rain,
to hold you close through love and pain.
Even on days I pull away,
my heart will find you, come what may.

Pragya Singh

Some hearts are not for you to know.

Echoes of an Empty Room

I thought I'd found a soul to stay,
a hand to hold through night and day.
A love so fierce, so pure, so bright,
a fire that warmed the coldest night.

But silence fell where laughter grew,
a shifting tide, a different hue.
One moment here, the next, a ghost,
a fading dream I clung to most.

I search the sky, I beg the stars,
"Was I not enough? Did I push too far?"
But heaven whispers, soft and low,
"Some hearts are not for you to know."

Now shadows dance where light once shone,
I'm left to heal, to stand alone.
Yet in this ache, I learn, I see,
that love must first belong to me.

Pragya Singh

A cycle carved in quiet pain.

A Heart's Unease

The echoes stir, a tale retold,
worn-out wounds in silence fold.
Patterns traced in sorrow's thread,
familiar ache, a path well-tread.
A whisper soft, yet sharp as glass,
shadows rising from the past.

The same old script, the same refrain,
a cycle carved in quiet pain.
The heart once whole, now bends, now sways,
lost in loops of yesterdays.
It flinches at a touch once kind,
ghosts of grief still intertwined.

Yet somewhere deep, a longing sighs,
to break the spell, to sever ties.
But hurt returns in careful art,
and weaves its weight upon the heart.
Still, hope flickers, frail but free,
a wish to end this history.

For even hearts that learn to ache,
can one day heal and never break.

Pragya Singh

I still chase the fireflies.

Glass House

They speak in sharp-edged certainties,
cold as steel, loud as war.
Their words don't bend, don't soften,
just crash like waves against my shore.

I hold the world in open palms,
wide-eyed, eager, full of light.
They call it foolish, call it fragile,
but I still chase the fireflies.

I laugh too loud, I dream too wildly,
still believe in "meant to be."
They roll their eyes at all my wonder,
but I won't let them weather me.

Let them be blunt, let them be bitter,
let their hearts turn hard as stone.
I'll stay a kid, I'll stay unshaken,
wearing love like it's my own.

Pragya Singh

We write only to empty the ache.

The Fear of Writing You

You still tease me
for the shadows I traced in ink,
ask if I lost myself in the echo of you.

But love,
I only ever whispered light, called you dawn,
held you like morning breath.
Strange how we never write joy,
only sorrow to keep it from settling too deep.

Now, I feel you slipping
into my silences, and I fear
you'll one day live
only in the lines I write to forget.

Pragya Singh

The past still lingers, just misplaced.

Graveyard of Echoes

The moon stoops low, a silver spy,
watching over names the world passed by.
Soft vines creep where whispers rest,
cradling stories time suppressed.

Fireflies flicker like stolen light,
dancing between the graves at night.
The wind hums secrets through the stones,
lost lullabies, hollow bones.

A teacup lingers, cracked and cold,
once held hands now dust and old.
An open book, its pages torn,
dreams half-written, left forlorn.

Thoughts drift up like autumn leaves,
soft-spun echoes no one grieves.
Here, where silence wears a face,
the past still lingers, just misplaced.

Pragya Singh

They toast to your victories with lips that have cursed your name.

False Embraces

They pull you in close,
arms wrapped like a promise.
Smiles stretching wide enough
to almost make you believe.

But most of the time,
the ones who give the tightest hugs
and the brightest smiles
are the same ones
who speak the worst of you
when you are not around.

They toast to your victories
with lips that have cursed your name.
They ask about your heart
with hands that have twisted the knife.

Yet you stand there,
letting them hold you,
as if their warmth
couldn't burn you too.

Pragya Singh

Your silence burned worse than their hate.

Silent Betrayal

I stood alone where shadows grew,
a quiet storm, unseen by you.
Their words like thorns against my skin,
yet you just smiled and let them win.

They mocked, they laughed, they cast me out,
their voices sharp, their whispers loud.
And you, my shelter, stood so still,
a vacant soul, a hollow will.

Did you not hear? Did you not see?
Or was their love worth more than me?
Your silence burned worse than their hate,
a choice unspoken, sealed my fate.

So now I walk with quiet grace,
no need for shields, no need for place.
For love that bends and will not stand,
is love that dies in trembling hands.

Pragya Singh

Some distances are measured in miles, others in the silence we are too afraid to break.

The Weight of Never

I know your blessings will carry me forward,
through storms, through silence,
to all the dreams I once whispered into the dark.

But still, I carry this weight,
a truth I can't outrun.
I will always feel like I lost
something sacred by never saying enough.

Because even now,
I cannot meet your eyes,
not in memory, not in prayer.
And maybe I never will.

Some distances aren't measured in miles,
but in the quiet between two hearts
that loved each other
but forgot how to speak.

Pragya Singh

You wore blame like borrowed velvet, and I still crowned
you in my rules.

Guilty & Golden

I held the truth like broken glass,
sharp enough to make me bleed.
You stood there framed in silver moonlight,
guilty hands, but soft in need.

I traced the cracks, the missing pieces,
found your footprints in the dust.
Every reason screamed to leave you,
but my heart still whispered trust.
Maybe love's not built for balance,
maybe justice bends for fools.

You wore blame like borrowed velvet,
and I still crowned you in my rules.
So I won't chase, I won't condemn you,
won't pretend I don't still care.
Some hearts ache in quiet loyalty,
some names linger in the air.

Pragya Singh

The scariest thing is not losing you, but imagining you
dancing in fields of dandelions that were never mine
to claim.

The Smile of Ignorance

Either the world is blind,
or I'm still just a child.
Oh, the way I feel your smile,
like sunlight slipping through a lie.

A quiet curve, so knowing, so painfully unknowing.
The devil lingers in its dim,
whispering meanings I fear to let in.

I never painted you in shades of deceit,
never traced you with suspicion's ink.
But then, a story unfolds behind a frame,
a picture that holds more questions than truth.

Is it all in my mind?
Or did you ever belong to me?
The scariest thing isn't losing you.
It's imagining you dancing in fields of dandelions
that were never mine to name.

You've assured me, adored me, loved me
but how do I quiet the whispers?
How do I unsee a smile
that never quite speaks my name?

Pragya Singh

No fire fights this creeping frost, no
warmth remains, just echoes lost

Frozen Threads

Once, our laughter lit the sky,
now silence lingers, passing by.
Threads once woven, strong and tight,
now hang loose in bitter night.

Your words feel distant, sharp as glass,
a winter chill that came to pass.
Eyes that knew me, warm and bright,
now glance away, avoid the light.
No fire fights this creeping frost,
no warmth remains, just echoes lost.

Not rage, not tears, not cries set free,
just quiet graves where love should be.
And so, we part, no grand goodbyes,
just empty hands and hollow ties.

Pragya Singh

Did you forget, or did you choose? A friend who mocks is a
friend to lose.

Echoes of Betrayal

You knew my wounds, the lines they traced,
yet still, you laughed with no hints of grace.
Not in whispers, not alone,
but where cold eyes turned me to stone.

Once, you swore you'd never stand,
beside the ones who scarred your hand.
Yet here you are, their voices blend,
your laughter cuts, just like them.

Did you forget, or did you choose?
A friend who mocks is a friend to lose.
No anger left, no plea, no fight,
just silence now, that stand in their light.

Pragya Singh

But even glass, though cracked and thin, holds the sunlight deep within.

Glass Bones, Silent Wars

Soft heart, open hands, a quiet plea,
molding myself for all who see.
Bending, breaking, shaping right,
yet never quite enough in sight.

Do they know me? Do they care?
Or just a shape that shifts for air?
A fleeting act, a hollow face,
judged for kindness, left in place.

Doubt lingers, a shadow tight.
Am I real or just polite?
But even glass, though cracked and thin,
holds the sunlight deep within.

Pragya Singh

Smile is a mask so socially trained it forgets what happiness felt like.

The Lie We Wear on Our Lips

I've come to realise, smiles
are the most disciplined liars we know.
They stretch wide when sadness gnaws at the gut.
They flash politely
when anger could burn rooms down.

When someone leaves, we smile.
Not because we're fine,
but because begging them to stay would be pathetic.
When you tell someone
about your little victory, they grin.
Not for you, but to lock away
their jealousy, their aching little failures.
It's never about joy.
It's about hiding what your eyes aren't allowed to say.

A smile is a mask so socially trained
it forgets what happiness felt like.
I've learned, it's only real when your eyes fold,
when your teeth peep shyly,
when your face forgets how to rehearse.
Anything less is costume.

Pragya Singh

Sometimes quiet feels safer.

If They Ever Win

If my miseries ever decided to take over my head,
I'll be gone.
Not with notes, not with dramatic exits,
not with someone to find me in time.

I'd just... stop showing up.
Like unread messages,
like old toothbrushes,
like the playlists we never finish.
You'd look for me
in places I left long before,
in old group photos,
in comments I forgot to reply to.

And no, it wouldn't be fair.
But it would be quiet.
And sometimes quiet feels safer
than holding your own head above water
every damn day.

Pragya Singh

SECTION II

Of Almosts and Ifs

This is the quiet ache of nearly,
of touches not taken.
Words caught in the throat,
and endings that never had a beginning.

Here, longing lingers like morning fog ,
not quite gone, not fully there.
The heart stutters in a language of maybes,
and hope writes itself in disappearing ink.

A love that was almost, but never felt right.

Mine Almost

You were never mine, not truly so,
yet somehow, you're the one I know.
A half-written verse, a song left undone,
a fire that burned but never saw sun.

The space you left is quiet, yet loud,
a name in the air, a face in the crowd.
A hand never held, yet still lingers tight,
a love that was almost, but never felt right.

How heavy it is, this love left untold,
a whisper of warmth in a world turned cold.

Pragya Singh

Love should never taste like ash.

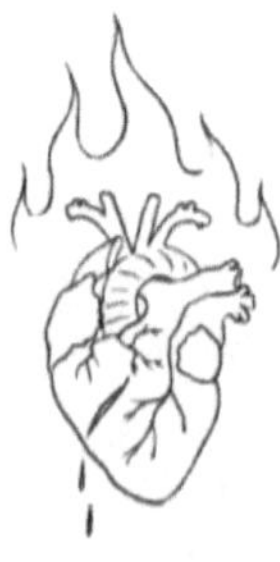

Love, Unanswered

She spoke his name like a whispered dream,
softly, to the ones who raised her right.
They smiled, they blessed, they held her close,
hope blooming in love's warm light.
She waited, patient, heart in hands,
for him to stand where she had stood.

To tell his mother, to call her his,
to choose their love, as she knew he should.
But he wove his reasons, thread by thread,
"Not now, not yet, my family bleeds."
And so she bore his silent storms,
tending wounds he swore he'd need.
She took his rage, his reckless words,
his shattered glass, his empty eyes.

For he was alone, for he was lost,
she let herself be the sacrifice.
Yet love should never taste like ash,
nor break the soul it claims to keep.
She loved him true, she loved him whole,
but love should never make one weep.

Pragya Singh

Too fragile to survive the dawn.

The spring That Never Came

Last night was a spring,
hearts blooming wild like untamed flowers,
laughter spilling golden,
soft as honey on warm, unguarded lips.

Smiles curled like petals in sleep,
held lightly between breaths.
But morning arrived too quietly,
the air too still,
the sky rinsed pale,
as if the night had never happened,
a dream too delicate to endure the sun.

Maybe it wasn't the world that changed,
maybe it was us,
the way we held it,
too gently, too carefully,
fearing that giving it a name
might make it disappear.

Pragya Singh

Effort is not measured in outcomes, but in the
refusal to stop moving forward.

If There Were a Story About Effort

It won't be about glory,
or the loud applause of the world.
It will be about quiet hands,
the ones that kept building in the dark,
when no one was watching.

It won't be about easy victories,
but the nights spent wrestling doubt,
the moments unseen,
when surrender felt nearer than hope.

It will be about trying, failing,
and trying again anyway
because effort isn't weighed in outcomes,
but in the brave refusal
to stop moving forward.

Pragya Singh

I built myself from all the wreckage.

Now You Watch

Funny how the tables turn,
how bridges burn
but shadows stay.

You walked away with sharpened reasons,
made me the villain, had your say.
Now you're a ghost in quiet corners,
haunting spaces you once swore to leave.
Watching close but never closer,
chasing echoes you couldn't keep.

See, I don't carve my name in ashes,
don't beg for hands that let me fall.
I built a home from all the ruin
and someone loves what you lost at all.

So watch, wonder, scroll through stills,
trace my laughter across your screen.
But some mistakes don't earn redemption.
Some doors don't reopen clean.

Pragya Singh

And maybe love was just the prelude

Headlines and Heartbreak

I was a secret he used like a weapon,
a quiet room turned into a stage.
Soft-lit whispers, hands in the dark,
now framed in fire, now set to a page.

She told the world with a trembling voice,
painted the picture, left out the gray.
Turned our echoes into a sermon,
turned my silence into her stage play.

I held her close, I held her quiet,
but truth's a script we rewrite in time.
She left with reasons she wouldn't whisper,
but screamed them loud like they weren't mine.

And maybe love was just the prelude,
maybe loss was meant to sell.
But when the crowd clears and night is quiet,
she'll hear my name, and know it well.

Pragya Singh

There are a thousand ways to cross over a woman's heart but you chose the shortcut.

The Easiest Way In

There are a thousand ways
to cross the bridge of a woman's heart.
Soft words, woven like poetry.
Hands that hold without asking.
Patience that lingers in silence.

But you chose the easiest route,
the shortcut, the well-worn trail,
a borrowed line, a practiced smile,
a fleeting touch dressed up as feeling.
And never once,
did you pause
to truly learn
the way.

Pragya Singh

While my mind played only you on a loop I couldn't sway.

Occupied by You

In the echoes of your lovely face,
I searched for songs to match the pace,
soft melodies, tender and slow,
but none could hum the ache I know.

You'll say I'm being dramatic,
that it's just another passing phase,
but every note just disappeared
while my mind played you, always.

Pragya Singh

If I am a shadow, then let me be free.

Where Do You Keep Me?

Where do you keep me, in light or in shade?
Am I a whisper, too fleeting to stay?

Do I live in your hands, in the warmth of your palm,
Or just in the echoes of words left unsaid?
Do you carve me in ink, do you dare speak my name?
Or am I a secret you hide in the rain?

Do I bloom in the open, for the world to see,
Or am I a ghost you only let be?
If I am a shadow, then let me be free,
For love in the dark is no love meant for me.

Pragya Singh

He loves you in glances, in fleeting smiles,
but words sometimes slip away.

Lost in Love

They say when a boy is truly in love,
his eyes will seek you in every crowd,
like a moth to a quiet flame,
like a wave drawn back to the moon's soft shroud.

And oh, he looks,
when he thinks you won't see,
when laughter slips through your lips,
when the wind plays with your hair so free.

But he is lost,
not in the way of love fading,
not in the way of careless hearts,
but like a dreamer still hesitating.

His mind is a sky full of static thoughts,
his silence, a song he can't yet play.
He loves you in glances, in fleeting smiles,
but words sometimes slip away.

You wonder if he sees you whole,
or if he's drifting in his own sea.
But love isn't always loud, my dear,
sometimes, it's just meant to be.

Pragya Singh

Maybe the beauty was always in the colors we never name.

The Colors We Choose

People paint themselves in extremes,
all shadow or bursting light.
As if the in-between
was never meant to exist.

But i have seen hearts
that hold both silence and song,
soft storms and quiet sunrises
never just one, never just whole.

Maybe we were never meant
to live in absolutes,
maybe the beauty was always
in the colors we never name.

Pragya Singh

Dreams may sleep, but they don't die.

Unwritten Pages

She traced her name on paper dreams,
a future stitched in quiet schemes.
Her hands once held the weight of books,
now they carry what life took.

The world was loud, the path was clear,
but duty whispered in her ear.
So she stepped back, she let it go,
watched the years drift soft and slow.

Yet in her heart, the pages turn,
the lessons wait, the embers burn.
For dreams may sleep, but they don't die,
they wait for wings, they wait to fly.

Pragya Singh

Love me not where sunlight sings,
But where the night folds broken wings.

Love Me at My Darkest

Love me not where sunlight sings,
but where the night folds broken wings.
Not in the glow of perfect days,
but where the silence holds its weight.

Love me when my voice is still,
when I am shadow, lost in will.
When I am winter, cold and deep,
a storm that even angels weep.

Do not fear the hollow ache,
the ruin, the wound, the heart that breaks.
For love that stays through ruin's call,
is love that never fades at all.

Pragya Singh

But love should bloom where all can see,
Not hide in corners, lost at sea.

A Love Unseen

I do not deserve the hollow wait,
the silent echoes at love's locked gate.
The moonlight fades, the stars stand still,
yet here I am, against my will.

Not knowing where your footsteps fall,
or if my name still lingers at all.
Not feeling warmth, nor hand in mine,
a ghost adrift in love's design.

Am I the whisper lost in air?
A fleeting glance, a half-meant stare?
To love in shadow, dim, confined,
a heart that aches, yet stays entwined.

But love should bloom where all can see,
not hide in corners, lost at sea.
So I will turn, let night make way,
for love that stays, for love that stays.

Pragya Singh

SECTION III

Of Becoming and Beliefs

Here is the slow unraveling,
and the even slower rising.
The self stitched together
with golden thread and firelight.

This is where we unlearn silence,
where we dare to speak the soft truths aloud.

Every line here is a step
from the ashes to the sky,
From being broken,
to becoming whole.

I am learning to stand where I once fell,
to turn my wounds into stories to tell.

Becoming

I am learning to stand where I once fell,
to turn my wounds into stories to tell.
The past still lingers, soft yet strong,
but I am not where I was for long.

I gather the light in broken hands,
watering hope where sorrow stands.
Each day, a step, however small,
each breath, a whisper, "I can, I will, I'll heal through all."

The rain may come, the winds may shake,
but I will bend, I will not break.
For growth is slow, but roots run deep,
and even scars are mine to keep.

I choose to bloom, I choose to rise,
to meet the sun with open eyes.
For life is waiting, wide and bright,
and I am stepping toward the light.

Pragya Singh

Alone, yet whole, no chains, no ties, just open
roads and endless skies.

They Say Delusion, I Call It Dream

I walk these streets, my own, my free,
a rhythm beats inside of me.
A city vast, a world so wide,
no hand to hold, just my own stride.

They said I wouldn't, said I'd stay,
but here I am, I've found my way.
Through neon lights and midnight air,
through quiet rooms and endless stairs.

I chase the dreams I once just spoke,
I build the life they thought a joke.
Each sunrise proves, each step I take,
I shape my fate, I bend, I make.

Alone, yet whole, no chains, no ties,
just open roads and endless skies.
I did the things they swore I'd lose
but here I stand, the life I choose.

Pragya Singh

Flames in my chest, a burning light, through every fall, I rise in spite.

Unstoppable

Flames in my chest, a burning light,
through every fall, I rise in spite.
Doubt may whisper, shadows creep,
but dreams don't bow, and fire runs deep.

I've heard the voices, cold and low,
"You can't, you won't, just let it go."
Yet every word, each bitter trace,
only fuels my fiercest chase.

No chains can hold, no storm can break,
I carve my path, I choose my fate.
For passion grows where fear should be,
and nothing stops what's meant to be.

Pragya Singh

There is strength in gentle hands, in whispered
words, in quiet stands.

Strength in Softness

There is strength in gentle hands,
in whispered words, in quiet stands.
Not every battle needs a sword,
not every fight needs to be roared.

Softness bends but does not break,
like waves that carve the hardest lake.
Like winds that shape the tallest tree,
like love that sets the weary free.

The world may call for steel and stone,
for hearts to harden, stand alone.
But strength is found in those who dare
to heal, to hope, to truly care.

Pragya Singh

Desire without direction is a fire without a path.

The Art of Control

Don't cage your heart,
let it feel, let it break, let it bloom.
Don't silence your mind,
let it wander, question, dream.

If you must control something,
let it be your hands,
your steps,
your choices.

For desire without direction
is just a fire
without a path.

The Art of Control

Pragya Singh

Tell your heart, it's over now, no more battles, lay it down.

Quiet the Storm

Tell your heart, it's over now,
no more battles, lay it down.
The war you fought was never yours,
yet you still closed every door.

Let the echoes turn to dust,
not every whisper speaks of trust.
Not every ache is meant to stay,
some ghosts fade when left that way.

Breathe in deep, feel the light,
not every story ends in fight.
You are doing, you are free,
happiness looks good on thee.

Pragya Singh

Freedom was never in the holding, but in
learning to release.

The Weight of Letting Go

Losing all expectation
felt like untying a knot.
Years spent pulling tighter,
then suddenly, the air grew lighter.

My hands uncurled,
my heart unburdened.

I learned,
freedom was never in the holding,
but in the grace
of letting go.

Pragya Singh

Maybe you don't need a heart to break, to feel the weight of what's at stake.

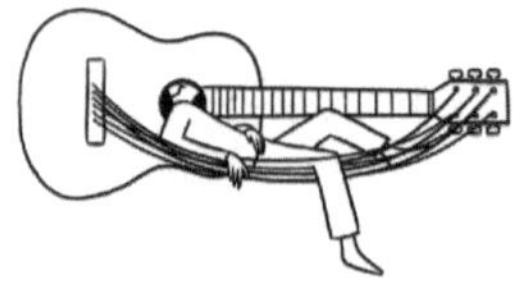

But I Still Felt It

Never had a heartbreak, never felt the sting,
never watched love turn to a ghost of a thing.
But when Taylor sings of losing grip,
why do I feel it, why does it hit?

Never had someone walk away,
never heard a love lie and betray.
Still, Back to December makes me ache,
and The Archer knows what I can't shake.

Maybe it's the way the chords unwind,
the way her words slip into mine.
Maybe you don't need a heart to break,
to feel the weight of what's at stake.

Pragya Singh

Healing comes not swift, nor kind,
but slow, like light that finds the blind.

Fragments

I stitched the wound with quiet hands,
threaded hope through broken strands.
But every step, each breath, each bend,
it splits apart, won't let me mend.

The air is thick with old goodbyes,
scars unspoken, laced with lies.
I press it closed, I beg, I pray,
yet cracks still bloom like dawn's first gray.

Perhaps the trick is not to fight,
not to seal the wound too tight.
But let it breathe, let it weep,
let pain run deep before it sleeps.

For even cracks, in time, may weave
a map of all that we believe.
And healing comes not swift, nor kind,
but slow, like light that finds the blind.

Pragya Singh

I root my soul in pages deep, where wisdom blooms and sorrows sleep.

Grounded Heart

With this heart of mine, I stand apart,
unmoved by the world's fleeting art.
I root my soul in pages deep,
where wisdom blooms and sorrows sleep.

In shaded words, I find my light,
a quiet truth, a love made right.
Not all the world's glow is true,
so I seek the good in pages new.

Pragya Singh

I built my dreams on borrowed skies, watched them burn, then watched them rise.

Ashes & Light

I built my dreams on borrowed skies,
watched them burn, then watched them rise.
Counted failures like old scars,
traced their lessons, made them stars.

The world was quick to shut the door,
to shake its head, to ask for more.
But silence taught what noise could not,
peace in things that time forgot.

I traded doubt for quiet knowing,
let wisdom be the seed I'm sowing.
For dreams don't die, they shift, they bend,
and knowledge stays when flames descend.

Pragya Singh

Maybe divinity is not in the sky, but in the way we rise.

Into the god element

I have walked through fire
and called it fate,
let storms reshape me
without asking why.

I have broken
and rebuilt with trembling hands,
yet still,
something greater held me upright.

Maybe divinity is not in the sky,
but in the quiet rise after the fall,
in the fierceness of love,
in the way we become
whole again.

Pragya Singh

Wear calm not as an aesthetic, but as armour.

The Ones Who Made It Out

If you meet people who treat themselves gently,
hold them close.
Not because they need you, they don't.
They've already carried their own bodies out of fire.

They were once shredded
by words they trusted, by hands they reached for,
by nights too long for a fragile heart.
They learned to be their own saviour
when no one showed up.
Now they wear calm not as an aesthetic,
but as armour.

Their boundaries aren't walls, they're lifelines.
They won't impress you,
won't fight for a space they don't want.
But they'll cheer for you
in rooms you're too scared to enter,
they'll sit with you in silence and somehow,
make it feel like company.

And if you're lucky enough to be loved by them,
know you've found a kind of rare peace
that no storm can steal.

Pragya Singh

I make destruction look like art.

The Dancing Devil

I must be the dancing devil.
How else do you explain this mess I call grace?
The way I twirl through disasters,
smiling like I planned the fire.
I ruin things with a rhythm,
break hearts like it's choreography.

And you, you still watch.
Maybe it's the way
I make destruction look like art,
or maybe you love a villain
when they bleed too.
I've never been the saint
never wore white
without spilling wine on it.

But I've always known
how to move in the dark,
how to laugh when it stings.
And if I must burn,
I'll dance in the flames like the devil
they warned you about.

Pragya Singh

Some wounds deserve to be felt slowly.

Mindful Even at Thorns

I've learned to be mindful even at thorns.
Not because it hurts less, but because some wounds
deserve to be felt slowly.
I don't flinch like I used to.
I let the prick sink in, name the pain,
watch it bleed, and then,
choose not to hate the rose.

Some things are meant to hurt
some lessons only grow in places that scratch you raw.
And I'd rather walk through them
with open eyes, with steady hands, than pretend
I was never cut at all.

Because pretending never made anyone stronger.
But carrying your ache like it's part of you,
that's a kind of holy.

Pragya Singh

SECTION IV

Of Love in All Its Forms

Love wears many faces.
It stirs in a cup of morning coffee,
lives in a grandfather's prayer,
hides in a trembling goodbye.

This section is a tribute,
to the loud loves and the quiet ones,
to the fierce, flawed, and forgiving.

It is about holding, letting go,
and the way love makes a home,
even in the hollow spaces.

A bloom of love in my little world.

My Spring

He's such a spring garden, fresh and new,
bathed in golden sunlight, kissed by dew.
The fragrance of heart in petals unfurled,
a bloom of love in my little world.

The brightness of my smile, soft and wide,
like cherry blossoms dancing in stride.
With every glance, a gentle breeze,
a whisper of love among the trees.

The calmness of pages, turning slow,
a love book read where tulips grow.
In his embrace, the season sings,
my heart in flight on butterfly wings.

Pragya Singh

For though the mind may seek to sever, the heart remembers, always, forever.

The Heart Remembers

The heart never forgets, though the mind may stray,
like rivers that carve through time's grand ballet.
Memories shimmer in twilight's embrace,
etched in the soul, no time can erase.

The mind builds fortresses, cold and tall,
locks every door, denies the call.
Yet love's soft whispers, like embers bright,
glow in the dark, defying the night.

A song, a scent, a fleeting place,
summons the past in a tender embrace.
For though the mind may seek to sever,
the heart remembers, always, forever.

Pragya Singh

With every drop, the world unfolds,
stories waiting to be told.

A Cup of Coffee in the Morning

The morning hums a quiet tune,
soft light spills across my room.
Sleep still lingers in my eyes,
as the coffee scent begins to rise.

A swirl of warmth in porcelain white,
golden rays and steam take flight.
First sip, a spark, a gentle start,
awakening mind, awakening heart.

Bitter notes and caramel streams,
a moment wrapped in silent dreams.
With every drop, the world unfolds,
stories waiting to be told.

So here I sit, embrace the day,
with coffee's touch to guide the way.

Pragya Singh

He trades his rest, his wants, his time, so I can chase what should be mine.

Love Unmatched

He wakes before the morning light,
hands calloused, knuckles tight.
Silent battles, unseen wars,
fighting for dreams that aren't even his.

But mine.
He stands where others turn away,
a shield, a voice, come what may.
When the world is cold, when hope runs thin,
he is the fire that burns within.

Every sacrifice, every scar,
a quiet prayer, a guiding star.
He trades his rest, his wants, his time,
so I can chase what should be mine.

And no love, no fleeting flame,
no whispered word, no lover's name.
Will ever stand as strong, as true,
as the love my father always knew.

Pragya Singh

So I pray, not for youth, nor days undone,
but for love to reach the hearts I've won.

An Old Longing

The chair creaks beneath my weight,
as dusk settles at my gate.
Once, these hands built, held, and fought,
now they tremble, worn and fraught.

I watch the world in hurried stride,
too fast, too loud, no place to hide.
The faces change, the voices blur,
and names slip past in winds that stir.

Yet love remains, though time is cruel,
a flickering light, a fragile jewel.
So I pray, not for youth, nor days undone,
but for love to reach the hearts I've won.

Let them laugh, let them dream,
let them chase the golden gleam.
And if they pause, just once to see,
may they remember a man like me.

Pragya Singh

It must be light, it must be free, a life that
breathes effortlessly.

How It Must Feel

It must feel like sunlight resting on skin,
not too fleeting, not too thin.
Like laughter echoing through open halls,
where every name is one that calls.

It must taste like a dream come true,
not distant, not out of view.
A table full, hands entwined,
hearts that never fall behind.

It must sound like a song well-known,
a melody stitched into bone.
No notes missing, no words unsaid,
only warmth where fear once tread.

It must be light, it must be free,
a life that breathes effortlessly.
A heart unburdened, a soul at ease,
like standing still... and feeling complete.

Pragya Singh

Not for the love he holds inside, but for how softly he
lets it hide.

The Boy No One Sees

He moves like sunlight through parted leaves,
soft and golden, yet easy to leave.
A kindness wrapped in quiet grace,
smiles gentle, never misplaced.

To all, he is warmth,
a fleeting delight,
a kindness given, then out of sight.
They take, they laugh, they never see,
the weight he carries silently.

But I know,
I see the words he cannot say,
the love he hides in careful ways.
Not out of fear, nor out of doubt,
but to keep the world from wearing it out.

And that is why he's precious to me,
not for the love he holds inside,
but for how softly he lets it hide.

Pragya Singh

They call her bright, they call her strong, but she only hears what could go wrong.

The Girl Who Shrinks

She stands before praise like a ghost in the wind,
soft and silent, folding within.
Hands behind her back, eyes to the floor,
as if kindness is something to be endured.

They call her bright, they call her strong,
but she only hears what could go wrong.
Every word, a weight misplaced,
too heavy to hold, too light to embrace.

For deep inside, a little girl waits,
sketching dreams on fragile slate.
She once reached high, she once believed,
before doubt taught her to recede.

But whispers remain, quiet and true,
the maps are still there, waiting for you.

Pragya Singh

I dare you to love me where shadows live, not for the light I give, but for the fire I fight.

Dare to Love

I dare you to love me, not in the light,
not where it's easy, not where it's bright.
But in the quiet, the restless, the deep,
where shadows linger and sorrows creep.

Love me in storms, in thunder's embrace,
when silence is heavy, too sharp to erase.
When laughter is distant, when joy feels untrue,
when I am a fire burning in blue.

Do not love softly, do not love tame,
do not make love a delicate game.
Love me like rivers carving through stone,
like roots that grip where wild winds have blown.

I dare you to love me, unshaken, unscarred,
to hold me when loving is heavy and hard.
For love that is gentle, yet fearless and free,
is the only love that was meant for me.

Pragya Singh

The scent of thunder before the rain, a force too fierce to be contained.

If Energies Were Perfume

Some would linger, soft and sweet,
a whisper of jasmine on summer streets.
A warmth that clings to skin and mind,
like love that lingers, slow and kind.

Some would burn, sharp and wild,
citrus-bright, electric, untamed.
The scent of thunder before the rain,
a force too fierce to be contained.

Others fade, a ghostly trace,
vanilla notes lost without a place.
A touch that stays but can't be found,
like echoes soft yet all around.

And some too heavy, thick with ache,
smoke and musk, the scent of weight.
A presence felt but never seen,
a memory caught in in-between.

If we were perfumes, what would we be?
A fleeting mist or eternity?

Pragya Singh

I mend their wounds, stitch their seams, but who will
quiet my own screams?

The Sadist Who Loves

A heart carved hollow, bruised and worn,
softened by fire, sharpened by scorn.
It knows the taste of shattered light,
of love that burned, of endless night.

Yet laughter spills like honeyed lies,
warmth woven into tired eyes.
Jokes like embers, soft and bright,
a flame for others, never mine.

They gather close, drawn to the glow,
never sensing the ache below.
I mend their wounds, stitch their seams,
but who will quiet my own screams?

For what is joy, if not a mask?
A gift I give, yet never ask.
And what is love, if not a game,
where I erase myself to keep them safe?

Pragya Singh

The red thread pulls, it ties, it binds, to hearts I touch but leave behind.

Tangled in Red

Lonely, but not longing,
lost, but never calling.
I walk through love like fleeting mist,
a touch, a glance, a moment kissed.

I chase, I fall, I turn to stone,
each time I swear I've found my own.
Yet I become the game I hate,
left behind, a twist of fate.

The red thread pulls, it ties, it binds,
to hearts I touch but leave behind.
I love them all, yet love no one,
a setting sun that meets no dawn.

Stuck between the past and new,
still tracing paths I thought I knew.
Yet deep inside, I crave the spark,
that tugs my thread and lights the dark.

Pragya Singh

Coffee was a peace treaty we both obeyed.

Bitter-Sweet With Two Sugars

We weren't a fancy latte kind of love.
We were filter coffee strong,
a little bitter, left to settle before you sip.

You took yours with two sugars,
I liked mine sharp,
like the kind my father made
on rainy evenings
when silence sat heavier than steam.

We didn't talk much,
but the cups knew.
Fingers brushing over brass tumblers,
arguments paused mid-sentence
because coffee was a peace treaty
we both obeyed.

I still make it sometimes,
leave an extra tumbler by mistake.
Muscle memory, or maybe grief
wears old habits like skin.
The bitter hits harder now.
Two sugars wouldn't fix it.

Pragya Singh

I watch this new reality parody my old daydreams.

Forgot Me Not Runaway

It wasn't a breakup, wasn't a divorce,
wasn't even a temporary space,
but something they forgot to name.
A silent rebellion against memories that cling
like wet cloth on a stormy skin.

You left not in footsteps
but in the way my mornings stopped mentioning you.
Not a message, not a fight, not a door left ajar,
just a skipped heartbeat on a regular Thursday.
I watch this new reality parody my old daydreams.
A bad sitcom where laughter tracks mock my grief.
I live in a rerun of a story I swore I'd never write.

Maybe you didn't leave.
Maybe I misplaced you
between 2 AM sighs and unsent paragraphs.
It wasn't a goodbye, not even a 'forget me',
just a 'forgot me not', wilting
somewhere between what we were
and what no one bothered to call us.

Pragya Singh

SECTION V

Of Solitude and Souls

These pages breathe with stillness,
where ghosts walk gently
and silence has a voice.

Here, the soul speaks without an armor,
of memory, of meaning,
of the spaces between what is and what was.

This is the soft weight of being alone
but not lonely,
of finding fragments of self
in the echoes.

But maybe soft was never heavy, maybe warm still gets
too cold.

Bittersweet Ghosts

I swore I saw her in the rearview,
a blur of lace and long goodbyes.
Streetlights flickered like they knew,
some things don't end, they just revise.

She traced her name into the window,
watched it fade into the cold.
Left her sweater on the table,
like a story half-retold.

And I was kind, I was steady,
carried love like it was gold.
But maybe soft was never heavy,
maybe warm still gets too cold.

Now the wind hums like a warning,
like it knew before I did.
Some hearts leave without a reason,
some good souls can't make them quit.

Pragya Singh

I'd rather walk alone in honesty than hold a hand that twists and ties.

Smoke and Mirrors

Smiles like satin, words like knives,
soft in the daylight, sharp in the night.
You toast to love, to bonds unbroken,
then whisper secrets out of sight.

I hear my name in rooms I don't enter,
laughter laced with something cruel.
You play the part, you play it well,
but I was never one to fool.

So keep your masks, your quiet grudges,
your half-truths wrapped in sugar lies.
I'd rather walk alone in honesty
than hold a hand that twists and ties.

Pragya Singh

To tell is to shatter, to break, to fall, so I carry it silent,
I carry it all.

The Quiet Weight

I walk with shadows stitched to my skin,
breathing in light, exhaling sin.
Smiles like glass, fragile and thin,
cracking beneath where the ache begins.

Happiness hums just out of reach,
a mirage I chase but cannot teach.
The sky is bright, the world moves fast,
yet I am stuck in echoes past.

Words knot tight behind my teeth,
a quiet storm I cannot speak.
To tell is to shatter, to break, to fall,
so I carry it silent, I carry it all.

Pragya Singh

Not then, not next, just in between, a life unlived, yet somehow seen.

Between Never and Now

The past hums low, a fractured song,
woven with chaos, stretched too long.
A storm of days, a restless tide,
where laughter and sorrow stood side by side.

The future flickers, a wavering light,
too distant to hold, too dim to fight.
It bends like mist, a fleeting breath,
a promise, a whisper, a shadow of death.

And here, this moment,
a hollow space,
too sharp to bear, too slow to erase.
Not then, not next, just in between,
a life unlived, yet somehow seen.

Pragya Singh

Sad for nothing, sad for all, a silent ache, a quiet fall.

As the World Unravels

The world unravels, thread by thread,
ashen skies where blue once bled.
Laughter echoes, hollow, thin,
a fleeting ghost beneath my skin.

Happiness, so light, so brief,
a dream that dances over grief.
Shame, a shadow laced with gold,
a story whispered, never told.

I know the stars, the way, the lore,
yet wander lost a little more.
Truths slip soft through open hands,
like tides that kiss and leave the sands.

Sad for nothing, sad for all,
a silent ache, a quiet fall.
Yet even as the night draws deep,
somewhere, hope still dares to keep.

Pragya Singh

A thread of light, a thread of me.

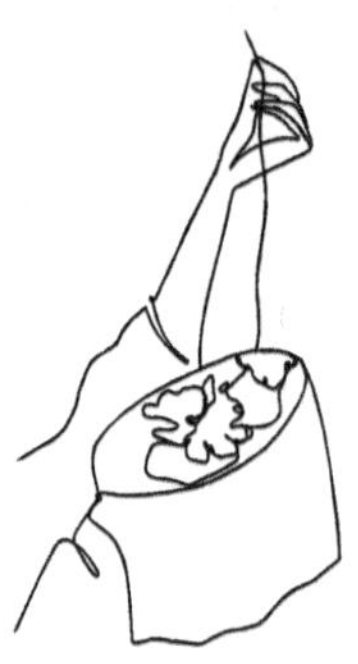

Fragments in the Fog

Autumn flowers, brittle and bold,
petals like parchment, stories untold.
Dried leaves crumble beneath lost steps,
whispers of yesterdays love-swept.

A mirror stands in the dim-lit hush,
blurred by time, veiled in dust.
It sways with ghosts of might-have-beens,
half-lit faces, half-felt sins.

The room is dark, the air stands still,
yet hope flickers on the windowsill.
A dream hums soft, stitched in seams,
a thread of light,
a thread of me.

Pragya Singh

A bird of dreams perches on the edge of dawn,
silent, weightless, half here, half gone.

The Flight of Elsewhere

A bird of dreams perches on the edge of dawn,
silent, weightless, half here, half gone.
Its wings catch whispers from the faraway,
stitched with longing, dust, and gray.

Dried roses rest where time once knelt,
fragrance lingering like something felt.
Once velvet-red, now paper-thin,
love's soft ruin folded in.

The sky spills gold, careless and wide,
a sun unmoved by hearts untied.
The garden hums, green and deep,
rooted in secrets the earth must keep.

And still, the bird lifts without a sound,
chasing something never found.

Pragya Singh

They walk past hearts like open windows.

Measured in Gold

They count worth in silk and silver,
in houses high and pockets deep.
They walk past hearts like open windows,
never wonder what they keep.

A name too plain, a home too quiet,
shoes that walked too many miles.
They watch, they weigh, they shake their heads,
never asking if I smile.

But I was raised in open sunlight,
where hands hold love, not coins or kings.
Where kindness isn't bought or bargained,
where laughter blooms in simple things.

So let them scoff, let them measure,
let them miss what they don't see.
For all their gold and all their grandeur,
they'll never own a heart like me.

Pragya Singh

He makes me laugh, like sunlit rain.

Innocent Blue

He makes me laugh, like sunlit rain,
soft and sudden, easing pain.
A love so pure, so light, so true,
yet guilt still lingers, painted blue.

The smallest quarrels, sharp and thin,
echo louder deep within.
Yet in his eyes, no storm remains,
only warmth that soothes the stains.

So let me hold this love with care,
not with weight too much to bear.
For laughter lingers longer still,
than fleeting words or restless will.

Pragya Singh

I crack the whip on my own grief, make it dance
so no one notices how tired it is.

Circus Master

I've been the circus master for too long.
Pulling strings, keeping the lions fed,
painting smiles on faces that forgot how.
I crack the whip on my own grief,
make it dance so no one notices how tired it is.

The crowd never cares who bleeds backstage,
as long as the show stays loud,
and the clowns keep falling just right.
I take a bow after every disaster,
like it was planned.
Even my sadness knows its cues now.

But some nights, when the tent folds in,
and the lights cut out, I wonder
who the performance was for.
Because the truth is, I don't remember
what it's like to sit in the audience.

Pragya Singh

Some gazes cut without ever meeting yours.

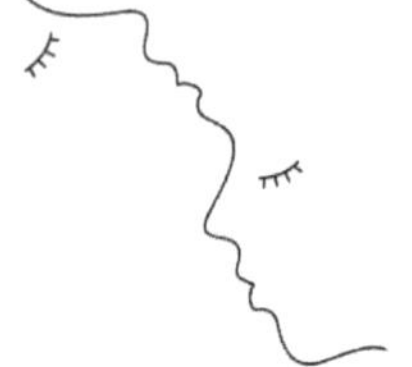

Language

Some gazes cut
without ever meeting yours.
An eye roll, not loud,
not cruel by definition,
but sharp enough to leave a mark
you'll nurse for years.

It's the kind of silence
that makes a room colder,
the smallest gesture that feels like
being erased without ceremony.

And the worst part is,
it's never loud enough
to call out.

Pragya Singh

You bleed quietly into other people's wars.

Empathy

The empathy isn't soft.
It's a burden stitched into people
who never asked for it.
It's carrying someone else's ache
like it's your own, feeling the heaviness
in a room no one else notices.

It's knowing which smile is fake,
which silence is a scream, which laughter is drowning.
It's crying for things that never happened to you.
Grieving people who won't grieve for you.
And the worst part?
No one claps for it.
No one says, "thank you for feeling this much."

You just bleed quietly into other people's wars,
patch their wounds, and leave
before they remember your name.
But you stay kind,
because you don't know how else to be.

Pragya Singh

Sometimes, love insists on being held.

More Than Flowers

He knew he couldn't afford beauty,
but love isn't something
you measure in currency.

He walked into a room
where flowers stood taller
than men like him,
their price tags heavier than his name.
Yet his heart counted differently,
each petal a promise,
each bloom a memory
he wanted her to keep.

He chose the one
his pocket couldn't cover,
because sometimes,
love insists on being held.

Pragya Singh

SECTION VI

Of Closure and Continuance

This is not the end ,
just the turning of a page.
A place where pain finds peace,
where we lay down what no longer serves.

These words are offerings,
to the you who survived,
to the you who is still becoming.
Here, the lemons bloom again.

Not bitter,
but bright with beginning.

Funny how some friendships shrink when one forgets
and one *still* waits.

When There's Time

You spoke of someday,
as if time were something you could schedule.
A better version of now,
waiting patiently for your arrival.

But your shoes are polished,
your sky is wide,
you've already made it,
yet you still hide.

I never asked for golden hours,
for perfect days or grand displays.
Just a moment, just a presence,
but you keep pushing that away.

And maybe time was never missing,
maybe I was just misplaced.
Funny how some friendships shrink
when one forgets and one still waits.

Pragya Singh

What we seek lives deep inside, not in the stars, not in the sea.

We Are All Searching

We are all searching, far and wide,
for something more, for a place to hide.
A touch of love, a dream so bright,
a flicker of hope in the darkest night.

We chase the stars, we chase the sea,
looking for who we're meant to be.
Through winding roads and paths unknown,
through silent nights, we walk alone.

Yet in the searching, we may find,
that what we seek lives deep inside.
Not in the stars, not in the sea,
but in our hearts, wild and free.

Pragya Singh

Like an angel woven into my bones, a voice that said, you're never alone.

The Angel Within

No matter how the storms have raged,
how the nights stretched long, unchanged.
There was always something, soft yet strong,
a whisper that pulled me along.

Through shattered hopes and quiet scars,
through dreams dimmed like falling stars.
An unseen hand, a steady light,
carrying me through the darkest nights.

Not fate, not luck, not mere chance
but strength that held me in its dance.
Like an angel woven into my bones,
a voice that said, You're never alone.

And so, I rise, again, again,
not broken, just bent by the wind.
For every fall, for every trial,
there was always something... and I survived.

Pragya Singh

Love is a whisper, soft on the skin.

What Is Love?

Love is a whisper, soft on the skin,
a forehead kiss in the hush of dim.
It lingers like dawn on the edge of night,
then fades like footsteps lost in flight.

One moment, hands held, worlds entwined,
promises spun like delicate twine.
The next, a name I've never heard,
written in texts, cherished in words.

Is love a flicker, a fleeting breath?
A touch that stays, yet walks to death?
Or is it a dream, too wild to tame,
melting between the truth and the name?

Pragya Singh

Like fragments of dreams that rise and fly.

Scattered Dreams

The stars are scattered across the sky,
like fragments of dreams that rise and fly.
Some shine bright, some fade away,
yet all still whisper night's ballet.

I reach for one, it slips my hand,
drifting far to distant lands.
Another lingers, soft and true,
a spark of hope in midnight's hue.

Like dreams I chase but cannot hold,
some turn silver, some stay gold.
Yet even those lost to the night,
still glow within, still burn with light.

Pragya Singh

Peace is not a place, but flight.

Fireflies & Dreams

Fireflies dance in midnight air,
soft as whispers, light as prayer.
Like fleeting sparks, they drift, they glow,
much like the dreams I'll never let go.

Goals like stars, distant, bright,
yet I chase them through the night.
With love beside me, hand in hand,
no fear, no doubt, just where we stand.

Peace is not a place, but flight,
a journey lit in golden light.
And like fireflies, small but free,
I'll shine, I'll soar, just watch and see.

Pragya Singh

If love is a tide, teach me the shore.

Teach Me How to Stay

If love is a tide, teach me the shore,
show me a place where I'm lost no more.
For I have been drifting, an ocean untamed,
afraid to be anchored, yet longing the same.

Teach me to stay when the winds start to rise,
when love is no longer a sweet, soft disguise.
When passion is quiet, yet steady and true,
when love isn't fire but something that grew.

If I am to stay, then show me the way,
make me believe that love doesn't decay.

Pragya Singh

If I'm the ghost when peace is made, then let
me be one in the wind.

The Middle & The Edge

I was the bridge when waters raged,
the name you called, the war you waged.
You stood on sides, but I stood still,
holding space against my will.

Every word, every tear,
I carried both, I held you near.
Yet when the storm fell into hush,
I faded quiet in the dust.

Now she looks with eyes unsure,
a stranger where a friend once stood.
Like I was just a passing shadow,
never meant to be understood.

So next time battle lines are drawn,
don't call my name, don't pull me in.
If I'm the ghost when peace is made,
then let me be one in the wind.

Pragya Singh

I spoke in flames, you heard in rain.

Whispers Unheard

I wove my words in golden thread,
hoping they'd shine in your mind, unread.
Yet, like echoes lost in hollow halls,
they crumbled soft against your walls.

Expectations, a fragile glass,
shattered quick as moments pass.
You saw reflections, bent and blurred,
misread my soul, mistranslated words.

A sigh became a silent storm,
a touch, mistaken, cold, forlorn.
I spoke in flames, you heard in rain,
drowned my meaning, left me pain.

Oh, how heavy the weight of air,
when meaning fades and hearts despair.
For nothing cuts like words untrue,
not spoken wrong, but lost on you.

Pragya Singh

I left the rooms that only loved me in ruins.

Good Sad Story

I was good when I was sad.
People liked me better when my voice cracked
and my eyes looked like
they hadn't slept since August.

I was good when I was breaking,
because broken people don't threaten anyone.
Then I healed, or at least pretended better.
Laughed at wrong times, started wearing colors again.
And they called it change.
The kind of word that sounds like an accusation.
"You've changed,"
as if I betrayed the version of me
they loved feeling better than.
As if happiness was a crime
someone like me shouldn't commit.

But here's the thing, I did change.
I left the rooms that only loved me in ruins.
And no,
I won't apologize for becoming someone
they can't pity anymore.

Pragya Singh

A vessel without a name can still hold something beautiful.

Vases Without Names

There's a vase in the corner of my room, empty.
But you wouldn't notice,
because emptiness is quieter than grief.
I bought it once,
thinking maybe one day there'd be flowers.

Not roses, not lilies,
not things that die too pretty,
but the kind of flowers someone leaves at a doorstep
when words run out.
I pass it every day.
The glass collects dust, like old promises do.
Is this naive? Is it lazy?
Or is it me still believing a vessel without a name
can still hold something beautiful?

Maybe you don't remember,
but vases can have flowers in them.
Even if it's just one marigold
bought with crumpled change
from a shop where no one asks your name.

Pragya Singh

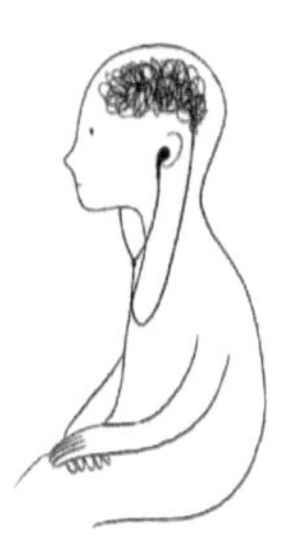

The weight of a sentence unspoken, hurts
more than the ones screamed into walls.

Unsaid, Unforgiven

Maybe it's cowardice.
Maybe it's a rebellion.
Maybe it's the most dangerous thing,
trusting silence.
I leave words half-stitched,
like wounds I refuse to dress.

Is this naive? Is this lazy?
Or is this you, quietly
walking me to the cliff's edge
and asking me to jump
just to see if I'd fly or fall?

Either way, I won't say it.
Not because I can't.
But because I know the weight of a sentence
unspoken hurts more
than the ones screamed into walls.

Pragya Singh

This book is a journey through longing, loss, and the quiet
resilience of the heart. To every soul who has ever loved fiercely
and felt deeply, you are seen, you are felt, and you are never alone
in your tenderness.
With love,
Pragya